STORIES OF THE
BIBLE

STORIES OF THE BIBLE

Creation

Drejervej 15,3 DK-2400 Copenhagen NV, Denmark
Tel.: (+45) 3531 0330 Fax: (+45) 3531 0334
E-mail: info@scanpublishing.dk
Website: www.scanpublishing.dk

Design by Ben Alex
Printed in China
ISBN 87 7247 770 9 (Hard cover)
ISBN 87 7247 766 0 (Soft cover)

STORIES OF THE BIBLE

CREATION

Genesis 1:1 - 2:3

Illustrations by
Gustavo Mazali

scandinavia

The beginning

In the beginning there was nothing—except for God.

God said, "Let there be light!" —and suddenly there was light all over.

Then God made the earth—the beautiful earth where we live.

God fills the earth

The earth was full of water, but God made land in the water and filled the land with rocks and dirt, plants and trees, valleys and mountains, rivers and fields. The earth was very beautiful.

God makes stars and planets

God filled the sky with stars and planets. He made the moon and the sun to give us light and warmth. Everything was in perfect balance.

God makes animals

Now God wanted to make animals - animals that swim, animals that run and jump. God even made animals that climb trees, and animals that fly high in the air! They all loved the earth, and God loved the animals He had made.

God makes people

Then God wanted to make friends. He created a man and a woman that looked like Himself. The man He called Adam, and the woman He called Eve. God enjoyed his friends very much.

The garden of Eden

God made a special garden for Adam and Eve. He called the garden Eden. In Eden, no one was upset, and no one was fearful. Eden was a friendly place, and God was very, very happy with what He had made.

Creation in the Bible

Then God said, „Let us make man in our image, in our likeness, and let them rule over the fish of the sea and the birds of the air, over the livestock, over all the earth, and over all the creatures that move along the ground."

So God created man in his own image,
in the image of God he created him;
male and female he created them.

God blessed them and said to them, „Be fruitful and increase in number; fill the earth and subdue it. Rule over the fish of the sea and the birds of the air and over every living creature that moves on the ground."

Then God said, „I give you every seed-bearing plant on the face of the whole earth and every tree that has fruit with seed in it. They will be yours for food. And to all the beasts of the earth and all the birds of the air and all the creatures that move on the ground—everything that has the breath of life in it—I give every green plant for food." And it was so.
Genesis 1:26-30